THIS COLORING BOOK BELONGS TO

____

____

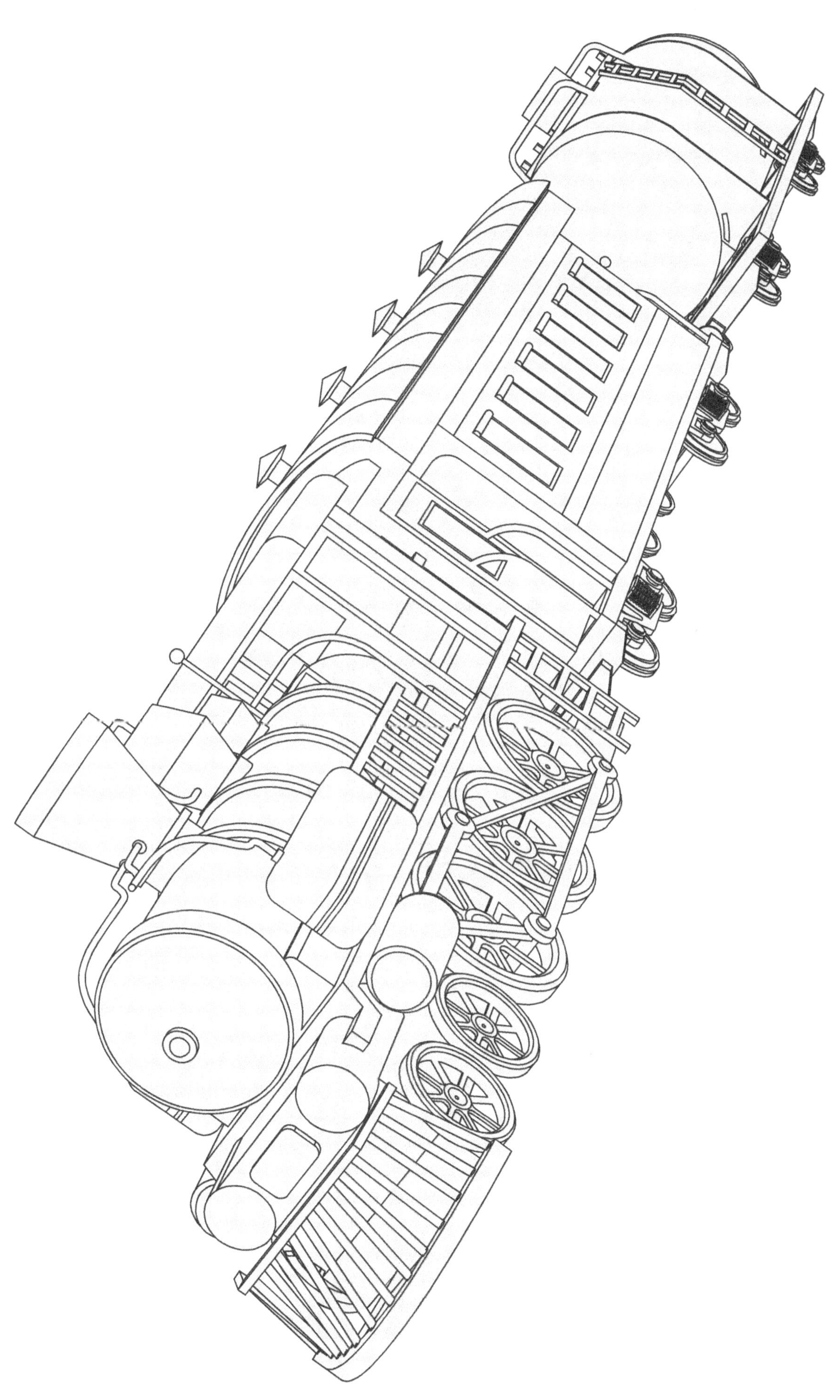

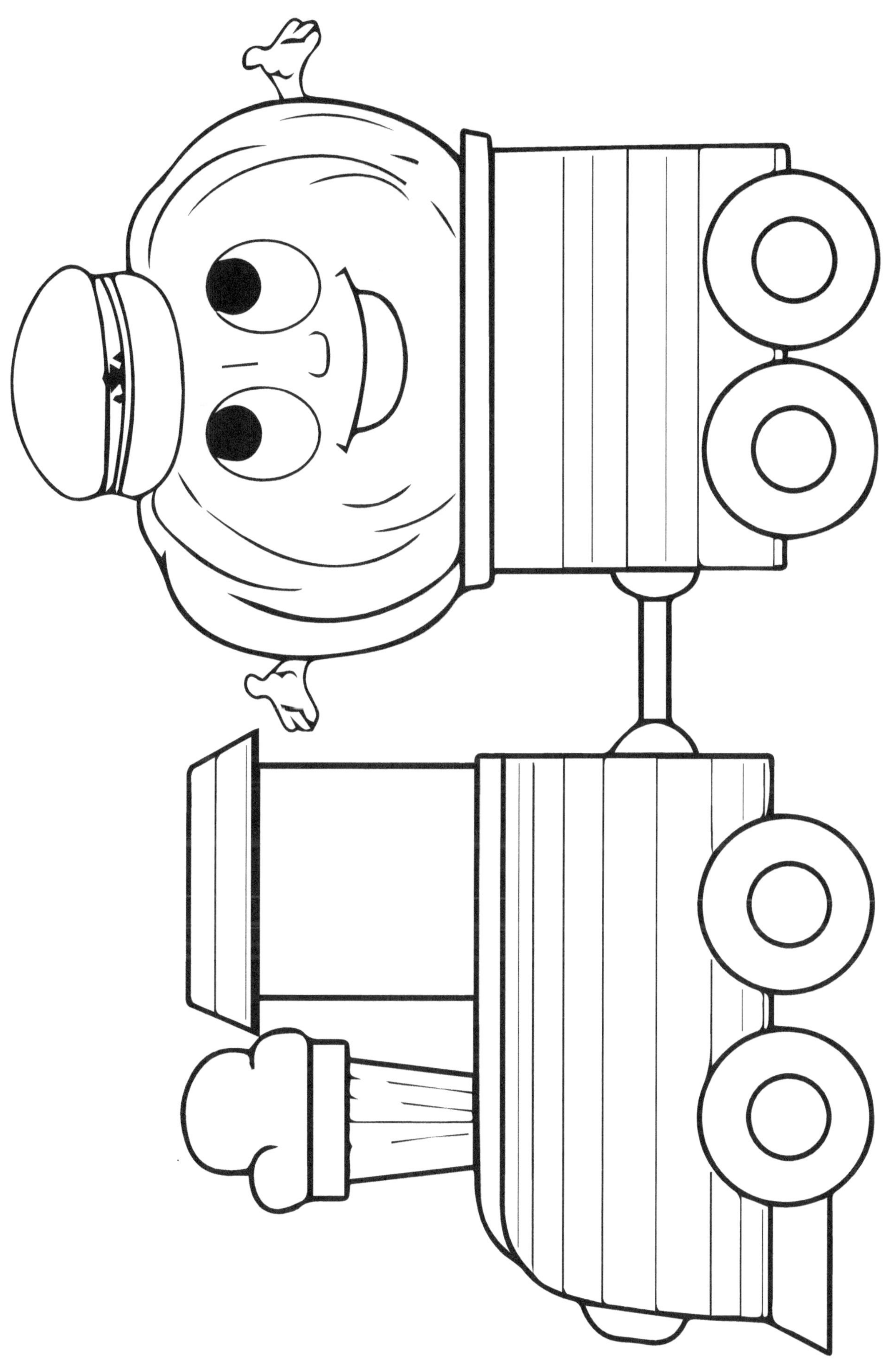

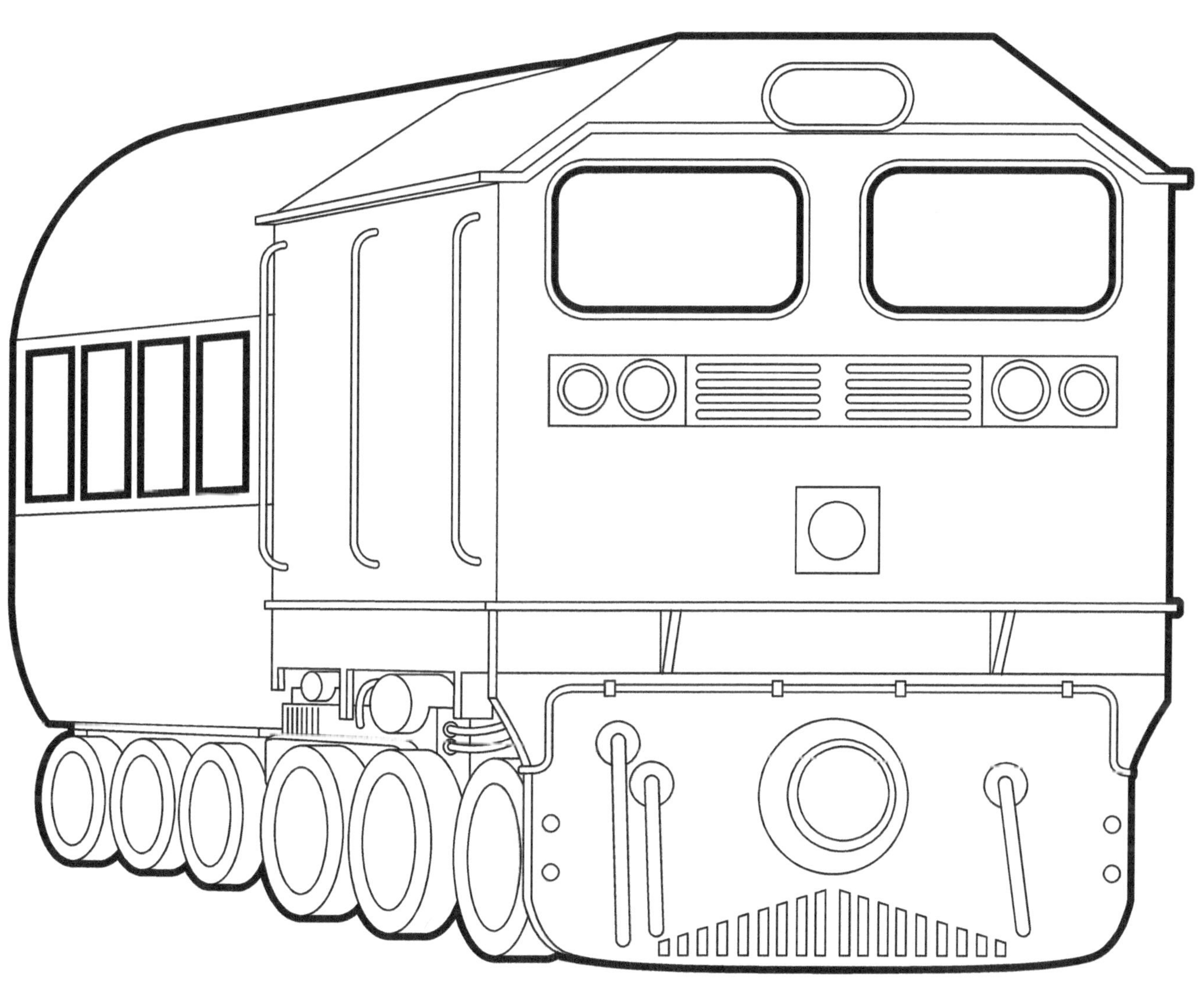

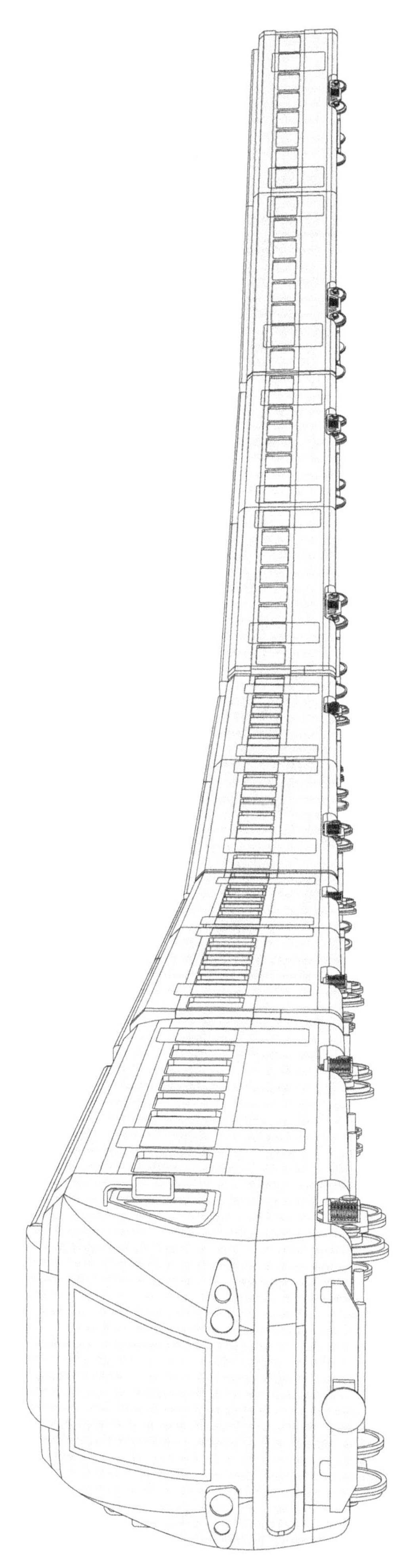

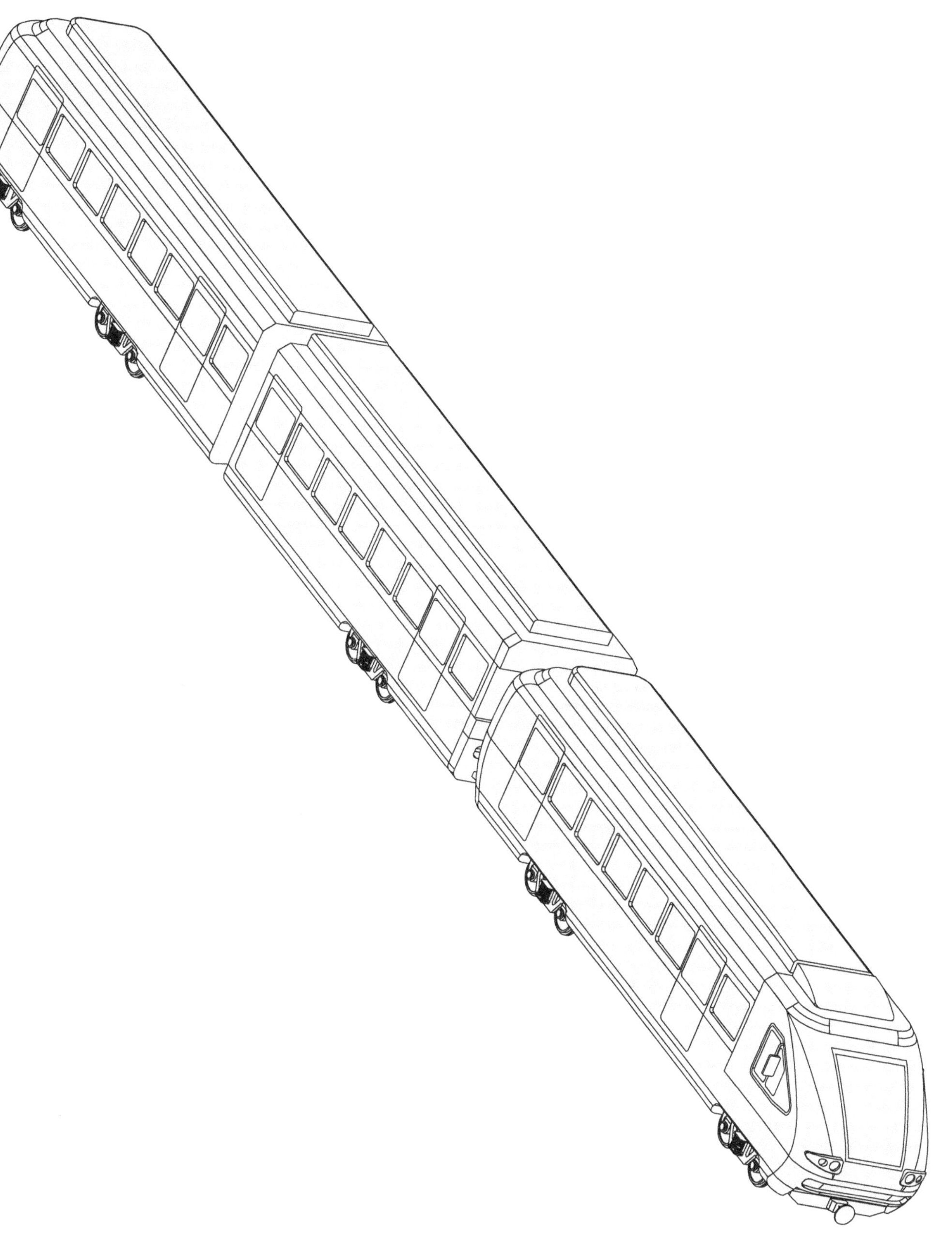

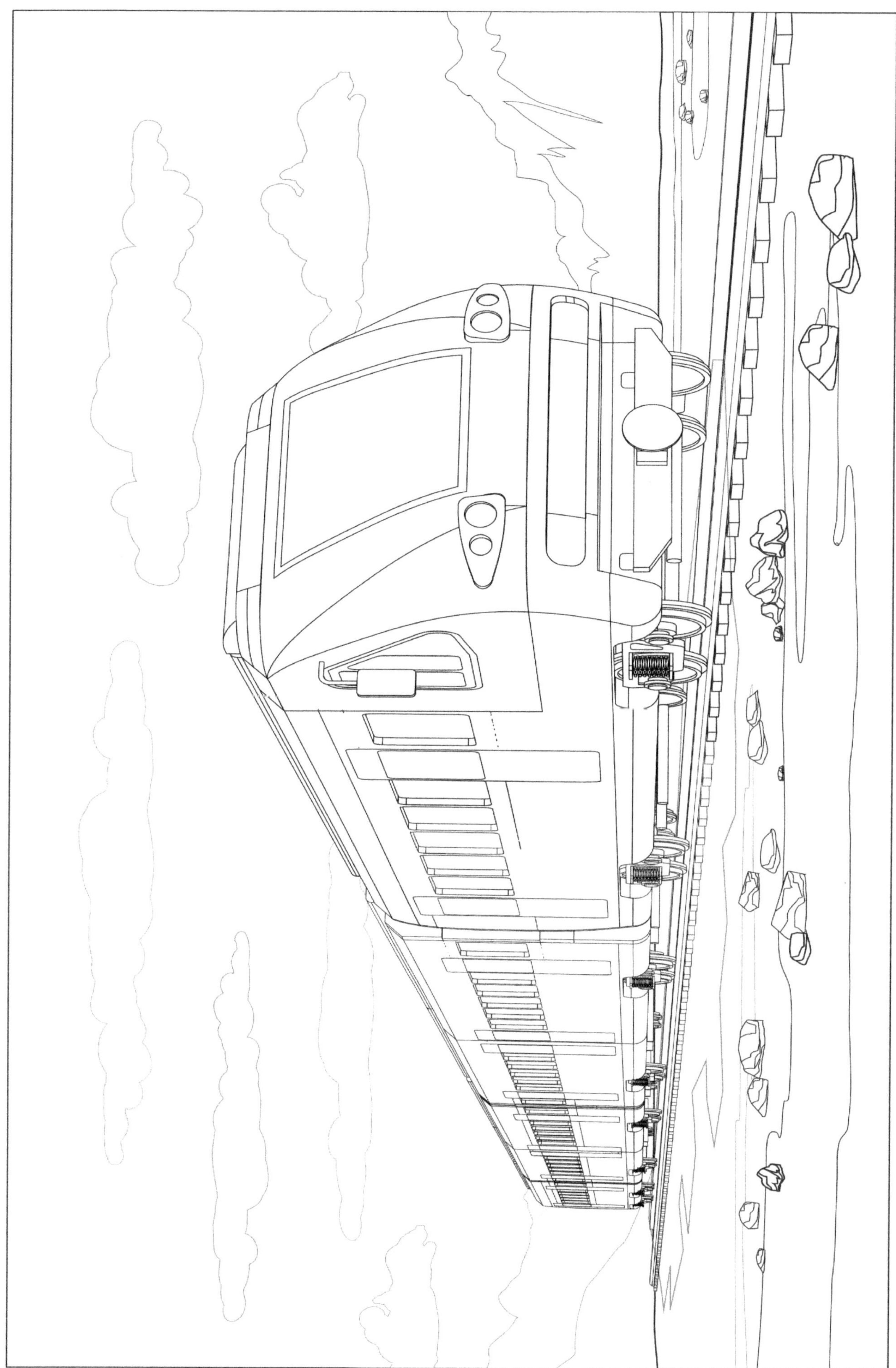

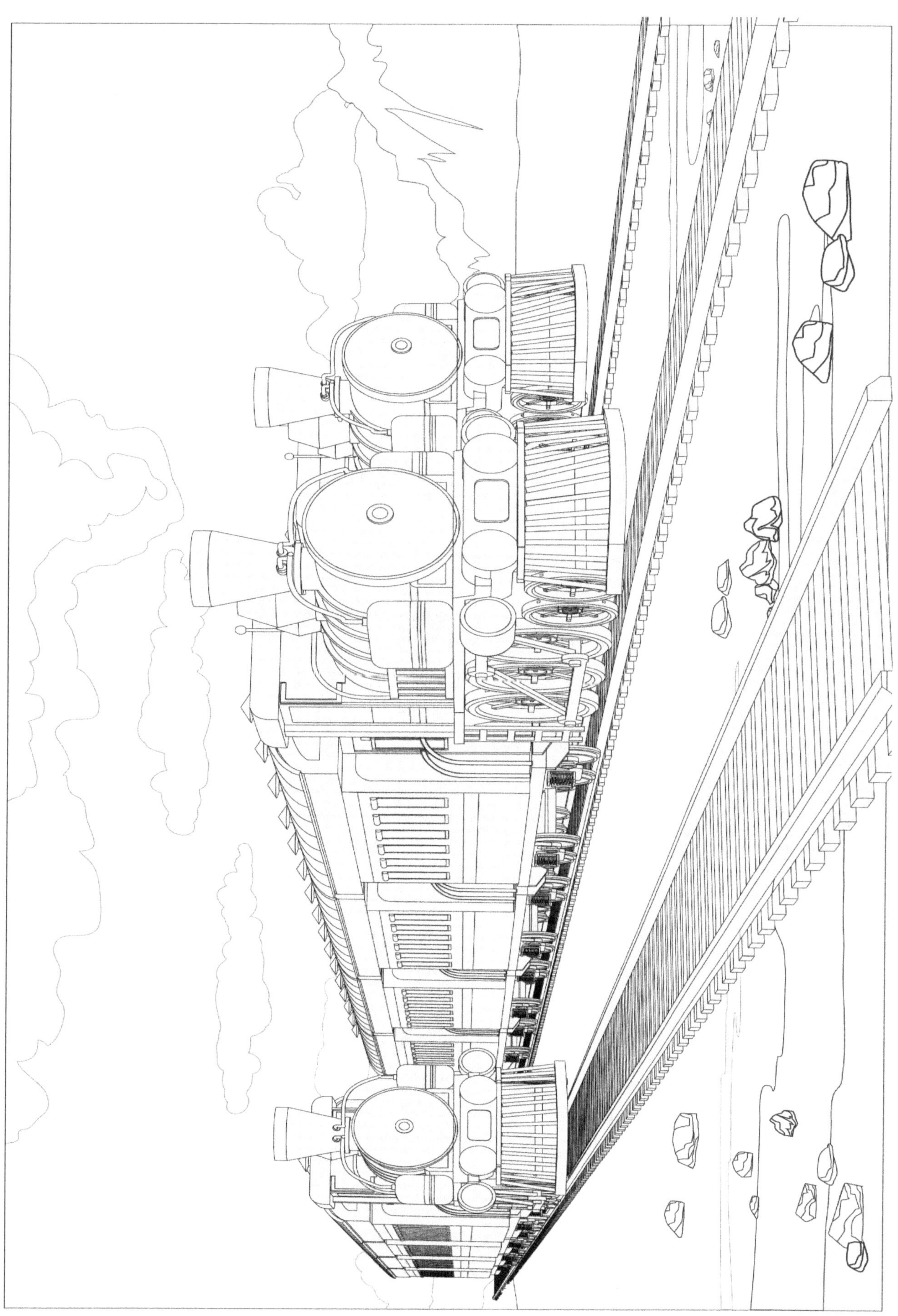

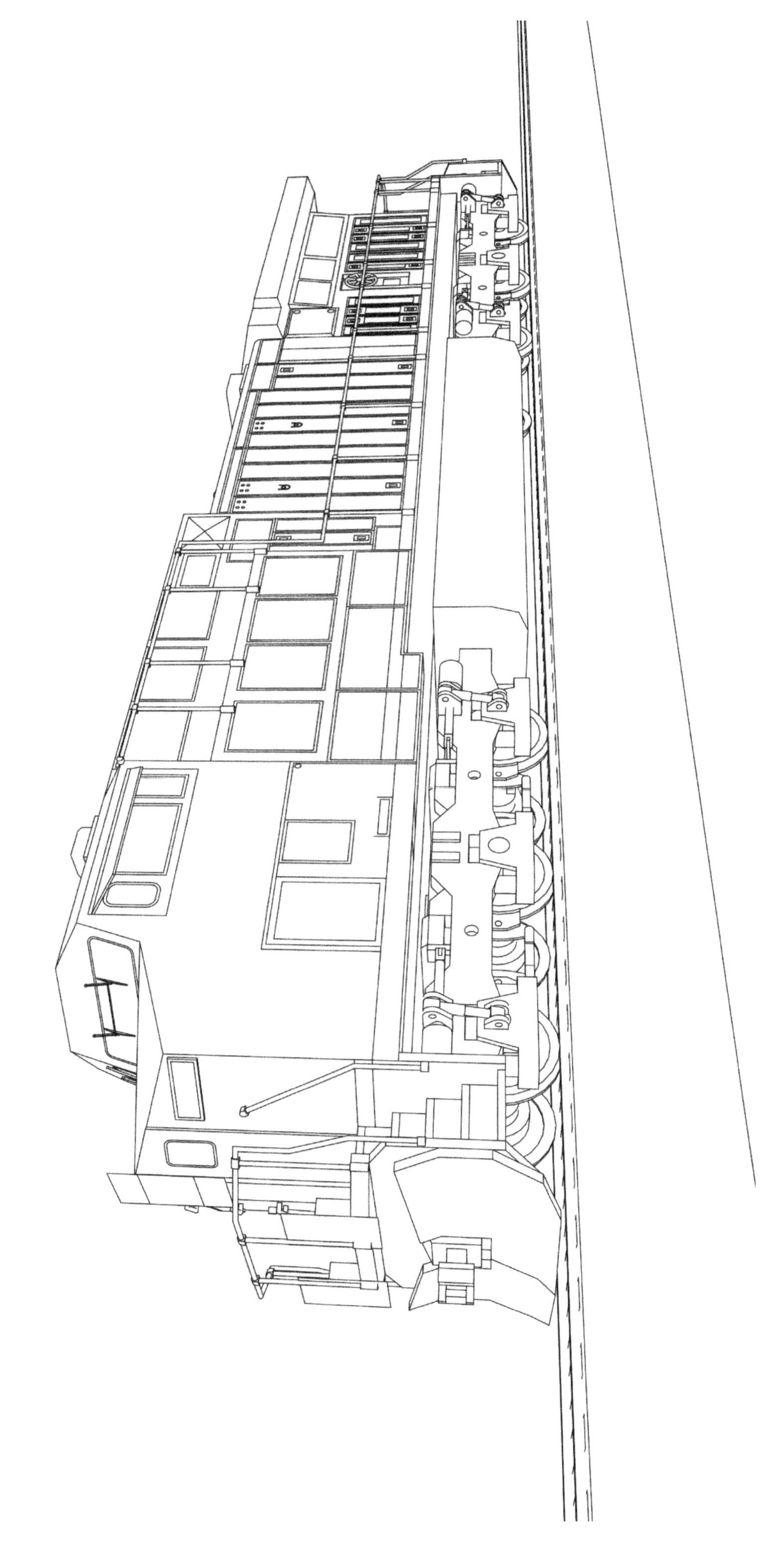

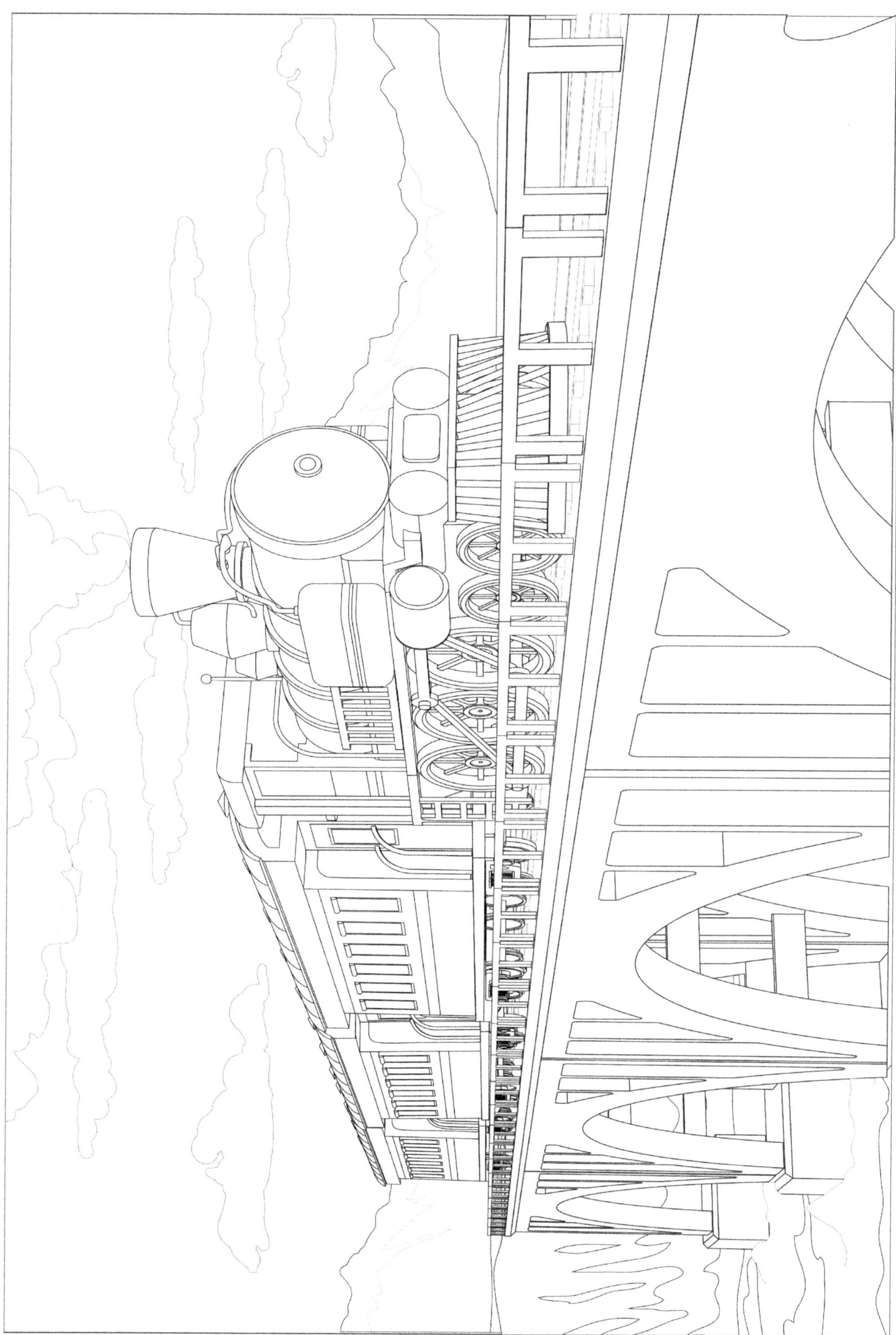

www.ingramcontent.com/pod-product-compliance
Lightning Source LLC
Chambersburg PA
CBHW081630250726
48657CB00009B/2816